The Fairey Swordfish was the Royal Navy's most effective torpedo-carrying aircraft throughout the Second World War. This sole flying specimen is with the Fleet Air Arm Historic Flight at Yeovilton, Somerset, and, for a time (as here), was painted with wartime invasion markings.

OLD AEROPLANES

David Ogilvy

Shire Publications Ltd

CONTENTS

Printed in Great Britain by C.I. Thomas & Sons (Haverfordwest) Ltd, Press Buildings, Merlins Bridge, Haverfordwest, Dyfed SA61 1XF.

COVER: *This Bristol F2B fighter was built in 1918 and flies today powered by the world's oldest working Rolls-Royce aero engine. It is one of the many rare aeroplanes in the Shuttleworth Collection.*

British Library Cataloguing in Publication data: Ogilvy, David 1929-. Old aeroplanes. Second edition. 1. Great Britain. Preserved aircraft. I. Title. 629.13334. ISBN 0-7478-0107-X.

ACKNOWLEDGEMENTS

The photographs on the following pages are acknowledged as follows: Air Portraits, cover, 1, 6 (upper), 11, 13 (upper), 17, 18, 19, 20, 23, 25; Brooklands Museum, 7 (lower); Dr Alan Curry, 22 (lower), 27 (lower); Ken Ellis, 27 (upper), 28 (lower); Fleet Air Arm Museum, 28 (upper); John Hoad, 14 (upper), 15, 22 (upper), 30 (upper); Stuart Howe, 29; Imperial War Museum, 6 (lower), 10 (lower), 12; Brian Robinson, 2, 24 (lower), 26 (all except top right); Mrs Olive Robinson, 26 (top right); Shuttleworth Collection, 3, 5, 7 (upper), 8, 10 (upper), 13 (lower), 14 (lower), 30 (lower); Torbay Aircraft Museum, 24 (upper).

NOTE: Although by aeronautical convention altitude is stated in feet and engine power in horsepower, they are given with their metric equivalents in this book for the benefit of readers unfamiliar with imperial units.

Percy Pilcher was one of the principal British pioneers of gliding. This original example of his Hawk glider of 1896 is in the Royal Scottish Museum in Edinburgh.

Aeroplanes became established before the horse ceased to be used as motive power; this pair has brought a Bleriot XI to a meeting.

THE BIRTH OF FLIGHT

There are many myths about early flight. The best known of these is the tale of Icarus, who is alleged to have flown so close to the sun that the wax of his wings melted, causing them to fall off. Very little technical knowledge is needed to prove the fallacy of this, for it is well known that the higher we climb, the colder is the air temperature. However, this and other stories draw attention to man's desire to fly and the likelihood that, one day, he would do so.

Knowledge of the theory of flight was at an advanced stage by the start of the nineteenth century. By 1804 George (later Sir George) Cayley was flying model aircraft of various shapes and sizes, with varying levels of success; but he established some positive principles of aerodynamics and he proved that on a cambered aerofoil (wing section) more lift is generated by the reduced air pressure on the upper surface, causing a suction effect, than from the increased pressure beneath. At that time no suitable power source was available and most early attempts were made with gliders, although there were some noted exceptions. These included Henson's 'Aerial Steam Carriage', which was developed as

a paper exercise in 1842, but which was not built; however, it incorporated several novel ideas, many of which bore fruit for others in later years.

One ambitious series of projects that emerged in physical form was the progressively developed range of Frost ornithopters. From 1868 onward these designs appeared, with flapping wings and control movements based entirely — and seemingly sensibly — on those of birds, which had proved so efficient and which we have been unable to match even today. L. P. Frost, whose work was carried out in Cambridge over eight years, taking the bird image to its limit, copied the wing pattern of the crow, scaling up the precise shape and position of each feather on the principle that if it worked so well for the crow it should do so equally well for him. He used steam as his source of power, with an Ahrbecker engine of 5 horsepower (3.7 kW) that weighed 110 pounds (50 kg), and the entire contraption was controlled with horse-style reins by the 'pilot' standing on the top. Frost's machine failed to fly, but in 1908 the Royal Aeronautical Society examined the design and declared that if the engine had produced more perform-

3

ance the combination should have worked successfully.

The first man-lifting aeroplanes that flew properly were gliders. No one could match the pioneering efforts of the German Otto Lilienthal, who flew successfully from 1891 onwards; development has since turned a complete circle, for Lilienthal hung beneath his machine, shifting his body and legs to move the centre of gravity and therefore achieving some manoeuvrability in roughly the same way as with weight-shift hang-gliders and some microlight aircraft today. To achieve positive control response more rapidly, however, he carried out several experiments with more conventional control surfaces, but in 1896 he was killed before he had developed these satisfactorily.

Other pioneer pilots flew gliders with some success and Percy Pilcher, a Scotsman, was flying regularly before the end of the nineteenth century. He designed and partially built a powered aeroplane and he might have achieved the first man-carrying powered flight, but he was killed in a glider whilst testing his ideas on the principles of flight. By this time the petrol engine had been developed, initially on a three-wheel motor carriage produced by Benz in 1885 and a year later on a four-stroke Daimler motorcycle, but designers' efforts to harness this new form of power for the aeroplane were thwarted by heavy weight and low output.

The Wright brothers, Wilbur and Orville, produced the first aeroplane to fly under power and under control by a pilot, but their step-by-step development programme that led to this has been overshadowed by the success of the first flight itself. In 1899 the Wrights were experimenting with a towed kite and they followed this with man-carrying gliders. Whilst conducting their tests without the use of power, they were running a parallel programme designing and building an engine and propellers, which revolved in opposing directions and were geared down to run at less than engine speed.

The Wrights also designed, manufactured and used their own wind tunnel. The first successful powered flight, at Kittyhawk, North Carolina, in December 1903, was therefore the result of serious research. Some cynics say that the Wright Flyer took to the air only because it used a launching rail, but this argument holds little weight.

The Wrights did not stop at making the first straight, controlled hop. Within a year they were flying complete circuits and in 1908 Wilbur took one of his machines to France, where he spurred the Europeans into more energetic action. Before then, European efforts had had very little success and the Americans were several years ahead.

Whilst design and development continued along the lines of what became accepted as the basis of a conventional layout, many people continued experiments with other ways of getting into the air. One novelty was the British Matchless, patented in 1909 by Arthur Phillips of Market Drayton in Shropshire, who was a bicycle manufacturer. This was one of the first ever 'convertiplanes', in which the propellers could be rotated in pitch to provide power for either vertical or horizontal flight. Phillips carried out several tethered tests with a motorcycle engine, but the intended two-stroke air-cooled rotary engine, which he designed, was not completed in time and the project was abandoned. The use of power that can be deflected vertically or horizontally has been tried throughout the development of the aeroplane and the Harrier is modern proof that the idea can work.

By this time several Britons were flying. Most of the true pioneer aviators designed, built, flew, crashed, rebuilt and flew again the results of their own ideas. Among the problems they faced were weight; structural strength to take the very different flying and landing loads; power and how to transmit it effectively via the design and speed of rotation of a propeller; shape, size and movement of the flying controls; and many other potential hazards; and after all these there was the problem of managing to control the machine if and when it left the ground.

Although there were almost as many ideas and shapes as there were people involved, certain design layouts became accepted and established. There were triplanes, biplanes and monoplanes, but

Often mechanics and helpers held back the aeroplane on the tail and elsewhere until the pilot was ready to move forward. This is a Bleriot XI at an early flying meeting.

for various reasons — not the least of which was the success of bird flight — many of the earliest machines were based on the monoplane. These machines were relatively flimsy and the wings were not self-supporting; normally a pylon above the pilot's cockpit carried wires down to the upper surfaces to take the sudden downloads when the aircraft landed, while wires stretching upwards from the undercarriage were attached to the wing undersides to take the upward loads when in flight. Whilst nearly all these early aeroplanes had conventional rudders and either elevators or all-moving tailplanes, many relied on twisting the entire outer portions of the wings to obtain any lateral or roll control. In these cases, when the pilot turned his wheel, cables would tighten or slacken to increase the angle on one side (causing it to lift) and decrease it on the other to make it go down. Known as wing-warping, this was an imprecise method of controlling bank and soon it was abandoned in favour of hinged controls on the wing, known as ailerons.

The very early machines could fly only when conditions were fully favourable. The weather needed to be almost calm and a cool temperature was preferred for obtaining as much power as possible from the inefficient, heavy and unreliable engines. For these reasons most pioneer pilots flew either early in the morning, which was particularly popular, or late in the evening. These machines were unmanageable for manoeuvring on the ground and helpers were needed in order to place an aeroplane in position for take-off; sometimes they held back on parts of the airframe to enable the pilot to build up power before they let go. To maintain directional control, it was essential to take-off into any wind there might be and also to land again in the same direction; this is because when it is on the ground an aeroplane acts as a weathervane and always heads itself into the wind. In practice, the problems of ground handling persisted on many types until the 1930s, when brakes became standard equipment.

The monoplane trend was especially strong in Europe, with many machines being made in France. Among these were the Bleriot that made the first crossing of the English Channel in July 1909 and the Deperdussin that followed a year later, undergoing extensive development for racing purposes. Both types, however, were used as trainers, with Hendon as one of the main operating bases. Britain was behind France in both aircraft design and piloting standards, but a successful pioneer was Robert Blackburn, whose first monoplane flew from the sands at Filey in North Yorkshire in 1910. After progressive improvement, by 1912 his seventh aeroplane appeared as a clean design with an acceptable performance. It flies today and is the oldest airworthy

One of the first successful British machines was the Blackburn monoplane of 1910. This later version flew from Filey in North Yorkshire in 1912 and is the oldest genuine original British aeroplane still flying.

British aeroplane in the world.

There were several exceptions to the monoplane trend and one successful British product was the remarkable Bristol Boxkite, developed from an earlier biplane design from France, although its inventor, Henry Farman, was an expatriate Englishman. The Boxkite was a strange sight in the sky, with a foreplane and a biplane tail, but despite its ungainly appearance it proved to be a commercial success for its makers; four were ordered by the War Office in 1911, when many politicians and senior officers were opposed to the introduction of the aeroplane, which, they insisted, could never replace the horse. Eight Boxkites were ordered for the Imperial Russian Army as the first export contract for British aircraft.

At about this time another pioneer was very active. This was A. V. Roe, who produced a series of triplanes with which he gained very valuable experience. Although these three-wingers were not put into production or offered for sale,

The Bleriot was one of the first aeroplanes used for artillery observation purposes and the large roundels on this specimen show clearly its military allegiance.

ABOVE: *A Farman biplane participating in the first British flying meeting, held at Blackpool in October 1909.*

BELOW: *A. V. Roe's first biplane preceded the famous Avro 504. It was the first aeroplane to fly at Brooklands and a replica has been built for the museum there.*

7

Most of the pilots and aircraft at the first two British flying meetings, at Blackpool and Doncaster, were French. Here Monsieur Rougier, wearing a dark suit and a bow tie, prepares to take off.

they were the forerunners of a long line of Avro aeroplanes extending to the more recent Shackleton and Vulcan.

Few people flew in the years before the First World War, but aeroplanes attracted the attention and interest of vast numbers. The first flying meetings in Britain, each lasting about a week in October 1909, were held in Doncaster and Blackpool, where daily midweek

Many early flights finished far from their intended destinations. This mishap, with the aircraft inverted on the sand, was the end of one pilot's attempt to fly across Europe in 1911.

attendances of between fifty thousand and eighty thousand spectators were recorded at each event.

The first pioneers aimed to achieve regular and sustained flight, with most competitions based on measured circuits of about 2 miles (3 km) and the corners marked by fixed pylons; highlights of the Blackpool and Doncaster gatherings were a machine climbing to 200 feet (60 m) in less than one full circuit, several flights exceeding thirty minutes in duration, an early night flight and the unusual sight of two aeroplanes in the air at the same time, but there are regular records of the crowds waiting patiently all day in the hope that the wind would drop sufficiently for some flying to take place shortly before dusk.

At this stage the aeroplane was just a flying machine. It served no practical purpose, but it developed quickly and before long it proved capable of considerable achievement as a fighting machine, which was a role very different from the one envisaged by those who first attempted to get into the air just for the challenge of doing so.

THE AEROPLANE GOES TO WAR

Despite fierce opposition from those who still thought of the horse as the principal medium of warfare, the aeroplane proved its value to an extent that could not be ignored. Balloons had been used as aerial observation platforms for ground gunners, but aeroplanes took over this duty about two years before the start of war in 1914. Bleriots and Boxkites were among the types used and they were unarmed, but before long individual initiatives brought aircraft into the fighting. At the start, aerial activity was in the care of the Air Battalion of the Royal Engineers, but in 1912 the Royal Flying Corps was formed, still as an army unit, while the navy operated its air arm independently as the Royal Naval Air Service.

Although wireless communication was tried experimentally in the earliest days, reliable lightweight sets were not available for regular use and more basic methods were adopted for passing information; message streamers were dropped for notifying the gunners of the enemy's whereabouts. Soon, however, revolvers and rifles were taken into the air and these led to personal duels between individual opponents. Hale bombs, weighing 20 pounds (9 kg) were released over the sides of cockpits and grenades were dropped on to enemy formations, but even darts (known as 'flechettes') were used, in the hope that large numbers descending on to troop concentrations would produce devastating results; the evidence suggests, however, that they achieved little success.

Serious air fighting required more effective weapons than the makeshift use of hand-held guns and soon experiments were made by fixing machine-guns to the aircraft's structure. The main drawback with these was the danger of a pilot firing into his own propeller and shattering it. At first deflector plates were fitted to the blades and any bullet that hit one of these would fly off in almost any direction, but by 1916 synchronising systems had been developed, by which the gun would fire only between the passage of the propeller. The best known of these were the Constantinesco (hydraulic) and the Sopwith-Kauper (mechanical) interrupter gears, which probably were the most significant contributions to the use of the aeroplane as an effective fighting machine. Dogfights occurred daily and several pilots became famous for their skill in these conflicts.

Whilst the equipment for use in the air was making rapid progress, so were the aeroplane and the aero engine. The rather flimsy braced monoplanes had given way to the biplane and there were several reasons for this: although an additional wing generated more wind resistance (or drag), this was not unduly critical at the relatively low speeds of the time and the extra lifting surfaces more than outweighed this disadvantage by enabling machines to carry the greater loads associated with military activities. Even more significant was the biplane's structural rigidity, for the pylons and wires of the monoplane were replaced by

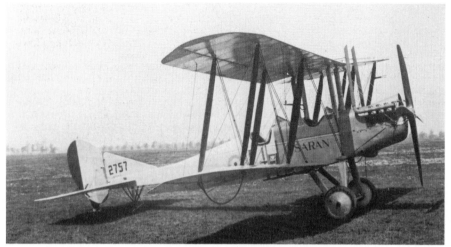

Even in the early days of the First World War, aeroplanes were bought for the national effort by communities. This BE2C was paid for by the state of Saran in India.

streamlined interplane struts near the wing tips and strong attachments to the fuselage at the inboard ends of the wings. Another advantage was the shorter span for a given weight-lifting capability; this reduced the resistance to roll and gener-ally improved manoeuvrability.

There were exceptions, however, and both monoplanes and triplanes played their part in the First World War. However, a remarkably standard pattern evolved and the majority of designs that

The Sopwith Pup scout of 1916, which served with both the Royal Naval Air Service and the Royal Flying Corps, had a le Rhone rotary engine on which the crankcase and cylinders revolved round a fixed crankshaft.

The Royal Aircraft Factory SE5A was one of the fastest, most manoeuvrable and successful single-seat fighters of the First World War. This specimen flies today with the Shuttleworth Collection.

proved themselves in action were single-engine tractor (that is, with the propeller at the front, pulling) biplanes, with two main wheels and tailskids and, for two-seaters, open cockpits in tandem.

One of the most unusual features of aircraft of this era was the rotary aero engine, used with outstanding success on a number of types. Unlike its static counterpart, the rotary had its crankshaft fixed to the aircraft structure with the crankcase and cylinders revolving round it. There was no carburettor as such; petrol was delivered via the hollow crankshaft and the fuel/air ratio was controlled by the pilot, with two side-by-side levers to enable him to achieve the required fine adjustment. This was critical, for an error either way would produce either a lean or a rich cut, the latter being especially serious, for once the engine had choked it was very reluctant to pick up again. To establish the best power settings for the day, a pilot would run up against the wheel chocks and make a mental note of the graded positions of the levers that produced optimum revolutions. Changes in temperature, pressure or humidity could alter the positions needed for obtaining the best performance.

Rotary engines acted as their own flywheels and ran remarkably smoothly, while the revolving cylinders helped with general cooling. However the heavy turning mass created an opposite reaction and the entire aeroplane had a tendency to roll against the direction in which the engine was rotating. This created handling problems on some types, especially on the famous Sopwith Camel single-seat scout (the term then used for a fighter), but it could be used to advantage during an air battle, for a machine could be manoeuvred rapidly to change heading one way. With so many moving parts, a rotary engine had a short operational life of fifty hours or so, but as aircraft losses were high, through both enemy action and accidents, this was not considered a serious restriction in first-line service. Power outputs varied from 80 horsepower (60 kW) for the le Rhone in the Sopwith Pup in 1916 to the Sopwith Snipe's 230 horsepower (172 kW) Bentley BR2 by September 1918. Before the end of the war in November 1918, however, normal static engines had been developed extensively and the rotary enjoyed only a brief period in the forefront, although the 110 horsepower (82 kW) le Rhone provided power for the Avro 504K trainer until the late 1920s.

Engines of many shapes and sizes were designed and built in the constant search

No. 1 Squadron of the Royal Flying Corps, later the Royal Air Force, with its complement of SE5A fighters in 1918.

for improved performance. Some failed completely, but among the more successful to see action were the French Hispano-Suiza and the Wolseley Viper, each of which produced 200 horsepower (150 kW) and was used in the Royal Aircraft Factory SE5A single-seat scout. With two forward-firing machine-guns, a Vickers on top of the fuselage and a Lewis above the wing centre section, the latter operated by a Bowden cable running to the cockpit, the SE achieved many victories, bringing fame to several pilots including Major J. McCudden and Captain Albert Ball VC.

Perhaps the most noteworthy engine of the time was the Rolls-Royce Falcon, which was one of a number of units used on the famous Bristol F2B fighter. Pressure for progress under wartime conditions led to the Falcon producing 275 horsepower (205 kW), compared to the mere 25 horsepower (19 kW) of the three-cylinder Anzani in the Bleriot only seven years earlier. The Falcon was liquid-cooled with a twelve-cylinder vee layout; this arrangement proved to be so successful that nearly all subsequent Rolls-Royce piston engines, including the famous Merlin of the Second World War and even the Griffon used in the post-war Avro Shackleton, retained this pattern.

In the very early days aero engines

were started without undue difficulty by hand-swinging the propellers, but as both size and power increased so did the difficulties. One person could not overcome the compressions of a Falcon and often three men pulled together, but this was uneconomic in the wartime labour shortage, so various starting aids were tried. The first of these to be wholly successful was the Hucks starter; this was a Ford Model T chassis, engine and gearbox on which was mounted the structure for the starting mechanism, comprising a long shaft that was driven by sprockets and a chain. At the front of the shaft was a crosshead, which would engage a dog in the propeller hub. When the appropriate gearbox drive was engaged the Hucks would turn the aircraft's engine, and when this fired the shaft could be disengaged telescopically against a spring. Many Model T Fords were converted to this role by the de Havilland company.

Although stories about aerial warfare during the First World War emphasise air-to-air combat, there were other operational activities. Reconnaissance techniques were developed beyond the initial task of spotting for the artillery and vital information was retrieved from the results of both vertical and oblique photography. The first planned bombing raid

The Bristol F2B fighter entered service on the Western Front in April 1917 and was highly effective with fixed forward firing and movable ring-mounted machine guns. This original example flies today with the Shuttleworth Collection.

was carried out in November 1914, when four Avro 504s attacked the Zeppelin works at Friedrichshafen and before the end of the war specialist bombers had been developed. The most significant of these was the Handley Page V/1500, which had four Rolls-Royce Eagle engines of 375 horsepower (280 kW) and a span of 126 feet (38 m). Its loaded weight was 30,000 pounds (13,600 kg). This had been designed to reach Berlin from bases in East Anglia and three of these large

The four-engined Handley Page V/1500 heavy bomber of 1918 was being prepared to bomb Berlin when the Armistice was signed.

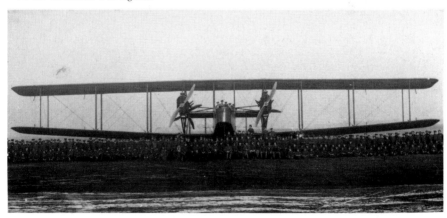

heavy bombers were being prepared for such an attack when the armistice was signed. Although the V/1500 cannot be credited with any operational achievements, it entered service in 1918 and was a notable example of the pace of aircraft development at a time of national need.

Although it is often thought that flying activity in the First World War was on a relatively small scale, more than eight thousand Avro 504s were built, and although accident rates were high, with frequent write-offs, in November 1918 the Royal Air Force (formed on 1st April that year) had 22,647 aeroplanes on its active strength. Fortunately, a few of these have survived to the present day.

ABOVE: *The BAC Drone provided very economical flying in the mid 1930s. This specimen is one of two survivors.*

BELOW: *After the 1914-18 war several military aircraft were converted for civilian use. This SE5A is equipped for smoke-writing.*

14

The Percival Gull was fast and provided cabin comfort. This example, now in the care of the Shuttleworth Collection, was used by Jean Batten for her many record flights in 1935-7.

STAGNATION BEFORE PROGRESS

With so many aircraft on strength at the end of hostilities in November 1918, large numbers were sold on to the civilian market at very low prices. Not all types were suitable to become revenue earners in commercial service, but certain aircraft proved themselves in specific roles. Perhaps the most noteworthy of these was the Avro 504K, which, as a trainer, was economical to operate. As a result, small operators sprang up all over Britain and wartime pilots were able to continue flying by providing pleasure trips. At 5 shillings for a local circuit, thousands of people made their first — and sometimes their only — flights in civilianised ex-service Avros. Although designed and built as two-seaters, individual initiative was not lacking where financial incentive was strong, so numerous 504s were converted to accommodate a total of three occupants and a few became four seaters!

Another aeroplane that had an extended life after release from military service was the SE5A. This, as a single-seat scout or fighter, had only limited civil use but proved to be well suited for aerial advertising in the form of skywriting. Major J. C. Savage was the main pioneer of this craft, for which his SEs were converted to take special smoke-producing chemicals in a fuselage tank, the contents of which could be fed at will into the hot exhaust gases. Names that remain well known today, including Persil and Players, were 'written' over appropriate areas such as seaside resorts and this proved to be a very worthwhile form of publicity; a well placed word in smoke, at the right height and in ideal weather conditions, could be seen over a radius of nearly 20 miles (32 km). In addition to their skywriting successes over Britain, eight SE5s were exported to the United States for a million-dollar contract with the American Tobacco Company. Other aircraft of this type were used for sporting purposes, participating successfully in numerous air races of the 1920s.

While former military types gave useful service with commercial companies and with individual owners, private and club flying could not make much progress until more economical designs were proved in practice. Even at this time the cost of petrol was considered to be a hindrance to expansion, so many minds were turned to producing machines that would travel as far as possible with the minimum consumption of fuel. Among the contenders were the diminutive de Havilland DH53 single-seat low-wing monoplane, which in the *Daily Mail* trials at Lympne in October 1923 achieved 59.3 miles (95 km) to the gallon behind a very troublesome 750 c.c. Douglas motorcycle engine; and the English Electric Wren, which used an ABC horizontal twin of only 398 c.c. and managed to fly 87.5 miles (141 km) on one gallon (4.5 litres). Although the DH53 saw small-scale production as a light communications aircraft for the RAF and two were specially equipped for hooking trials with the airship R-33 (one achieving the first successful release and re-engagement on 4th December 1925), these very low-powered machines could be flown only in favourable weather and their overall performance was too marginal for serious cross-country work.

After a not wholly successful attempt to build and sell a much larger and heavier aeroplane for the private market, the DH51, the de Havilland company produced a compromise that was an immediate success. In February 1925 the DH60, the first in a long line of Moths, flew from Stag Lane aerodrome, Edgware, and later that year this type equipped the London Aeroplane Club, the Newcastle Aero Club, the Midland Aero Club and the Yorkshire Aeroplane Club. For the first time since manned powered flight had begun twenty-two years previously, here was a machine that flew well, with an adequate performance and an economy of operation to bring flying within practical reach of many people. It was because of the Moth that the club and private flying movement became established.

Apart from their successes in Britain, Moths sold all over the world and versions were produced under licence in Australia and Finland, while later variants were built in France and the United States. The DH60 was everywhere: Alan (later Sir Alan) Cobham flew the prototype 1000 miles (1600 km) from Croydon to Zurich and back in a day; Moths won the King's Cup air races in 1926 and 1927; another climbed to 17,283 feet (5268 m) to establish an altitude record for light aeroplanes; Amy

Johnson flew a DH60G Gipsy Moth to Australia. The achievements were numerous and eventually the design was developed into the DH82 Tiger Moth, which became the standard trainer in the RAF from the early 1930s until after the Second World War; altogether about 7,300 Tiger Moths were built and many of these operated with civil flying clubs both before and after the war.

This was the era of record breaking. Apart from the many Moth achievements, other British light aircraft led the world in long-distance flights. In 1935 Jean Batten flew her Percival Gull-Six, a cabin monoplane powered by a 200 horsepower (150 kW) de Havilland Gipsy Six engine and capable of cruising at a creditable 160 miles (257 km) per hour, from England to Brazil (with a solo crossing of the South Atlantic in 13 hours 15 minutes), and in the following year she completed the first ever flight from England to New Zealand in 11 days and 45 minutes.

Perhaps the most significant of all the successes was the the de Havilland DH88 Comet of 1934, which must not be confused with the much later and larger DH106 airliner of the same name. The original Comet was designed, built and flown in a total time of under nine months to provide an effective British entry in the Macrobertson Air Race from England to Australia. At that time the state of Victoria was planning events to mark its forthcoming one hundredth anniversary and Australia's isolation from England in time terms was the reason for the contest. Entries came from all over the world, with aircraft of United States origin showing the most advanced features, but de Havilland refused to be beaten and three Comets were produced on time. It was the first British aeroplane to have variable-pitch propellers, flaps and a retractable undercarriage, while to obtain maximum performance from relatively low-powered engines the wing needed to be very thin and a new method of stressed skin construction was used. There were many problems, including undercarriage failures, and during the last night before the race all three machines had larger oil tanks fitted.

One of the Comets won the event,

ABOVE: *Some organisations keep historic aeroplanes in flying condition and this DH51 of 1924 is the world's oldest airworthy aircraft of de Havilland origin. It is with the Shuttleworth Collection.*

BELOW: *Three early de Havilland types in a flying display at Old Warden : the DH51 of 1924 and two versions of the DH60 Moth, the original of which flew in 1925.*

reaching Melbourne from Mildenhall in 70 hours 54 minutes; another DH88 gained fourth place. Such was the impact on the world that almost immediately the major airlines were spurred into action to reduce the times on their hitherto lumbering schedules, while only two months after the event Imperial Airways launched its first all-airmail service from England to Australia. The Comet was designed solely for speed and range and had no worthwhile carrying capacity, and no commercially viable aircraft could be expected to operate to such tight timings, but had it not been for this British winner airline operators would have been unlikely to strive to accelerate their services.

Military aeroplanes made relatively little progress in the years following the First World War. No major conflict with any significant nation was foreseen and the defence budget was trimmed to the bone, to the extent that for two and a half years from April 1920 No. 25 Squadron, with aging Sopwith Snipes, was the RAF's only fighter unit to defend the whole of Britain. Development generally

LEFT: *This Percival Mew Gull single-seat racing aircraft established several records in the late 1930s. Extensively rebuilt, it is one of a number of old aeroplanes in private ownership.*
BELOW: *In the mid 1930s the RAF was equipped with a wide range of Hawker biplanes including the Hawker Hind light bomber. This specimen is in the Shuttleworth flying fleet.*

consisted of little more than progressive increases in engine power and a gradual change from wooden to metal construction. For nearly twenty years following the war, nearly all Service aircraft were biplanes, with open cockpits, fixed undercarriages and fixed-pitch propellers.

Most units were equipped with examples of the Hawker range, with single-seat Furies as fighters and two-seat Hart variants (including the Hind) on day bombing, army co-operation and general duties. The heavy bombers were slow, cumbersome twin-engine biplanes such as the Vickers Virginia and, a little later, the Handley Page Heyford; the Virginia, although remaining in limited second-line service until 1941, had a top speed of only about 108 miles (174 km) per hour, representing a performance increase of less than 10 per cent over that of the V/1500 of 1918.

Suitable operational aircraft were few in number and there had been only small improvements in related techniques such as night bombing, bad weather navigation and submarine detection. However, in the second half of the 1930s a formal expansion scheme was established and only then did the monoplane return to the fore. Copious struts, wires and pylons were no longer needed for by this time the wing structure was self-contained, with the spars, ribs and stressed skin metal covering taking all the loads.

Although the first monoplanes to enter squadron service were very basic, progress was rapid. The Avro Anson coastal reconnaissance machine, introduced in 1936, had fixed-pitch propellers and the undercarriage was retracted manually by a long process of handle winding, so on short flights the wheels were left down; even when in the up position, they protruded sufficiently to cause minimum embarrassment if a pilot forgot or for some other reason failed to lower them. The cabin was noisy and draughty but the biggest change yet in design thinking was permanent.

From 1937, the Fairey Battle single-engine light bomber, the heavier twin-engine Bristol Blenheim and the even larger Armstrong-Whitworth Whitley were introduced in increasing numbers in offensive roles, followed a year later by the highly successful Vickers Wellington bomber, but the most noticeable transition was with the fighters. The famous Fury, the Gloster Gauntlet and the later Gloster Gladiator — the RAF's last

The RAF's last biplane fighter was the Gloster Gladiator of 1937 and today this is the world's only flying specimen.

ABOVE: *The Hawker Hurricane monoplane of 1937 with its retractable undercarriage and flaps (here seen lowered) was the start of a new era in fighters. This preserved specimen has been on the strength of the RAF Battle of Britain Memorial Flight for many years.*

BELOW: *In June 1938 the Supermarine Spitfire followed the Hurricane into RAF service. In 1958 only one was flying; today fifteen are airworthy and at least three more are being rebuilt.*

biplane fighter — gave way quickly to the Hawker Hurricane (which equipped No. 111 Squadron from December 1937), to be followed within eight months by the Supermarine Spitfire. Both these types began with large two-blade fixed-pitch propellers, but very quickly these were replaced by controllable-pitch units and the transition was complete.

The Spitfire has earned fame and respect for its part in winning the Battle of Britain, but more Hurricanes than Spitfires took part and they shot down a greater number of enemy aircraft. Hawker's tough, reliable and manoeuvrable fighter failed to grasp the public imagination to the same extent as the sleeker Spitfire, but it underwent relatively little

subsequent development and by the middle of the Second World War the type had changed its primary duty from defence to tank-busting and other low-level attack work. The Spitfire was unique as the only operational aeroplane to have remained in continuous production before, during and even just after the war. The design offered considerable scope for performance improvement and twenty-four different marks emerged from the drawing board, the 2050 horsepower (1529 kW) of the final version offering roughly double the output of those that joined the squadrons in 1938. Altogether 20,351 Spitfires were built for the RAF. British-built Hurricanes totalled 12,780.

The pressure brought about by the

ABOVE: *At the start of the Second World War the Vickers Wellington was the RAF's main bomber. Unlike most operational aircraft, which were all metal, the Wellington was entirely fabric covered.*

BELOW: *The first of the three types of four-engine bomber to enter RAF service in the Second World War was the Short Stirling. Although it was the least successful, it served well on many other duties.*

national need in wartime produced rapid changes. For heavier long-range bombers, capable of carrying effective offensive loads well into enemy territory, machines powered with four engines were required. The first of these to enter operational service in the Second World War was the Short Stirling, but it suffered from bomb-load limitations and a restricted ability to climb to a safe height; the Handley Page Halifax outmoded it and was the first to bomb Germany, attacking Hamburg on 12th-13th March 1941. The third and last type to join the squadrons was the Avro Lancaster; in the purely bombing role (Halifaxes and Stirlings carried out other duties, such as glider towing) it outshone the others,

dropping 608,617 tons of bombs compared with 227,610 released by the Halifax. The Lancaster outlasted the others by remaining in use on coastal reconnaissance duties for nearly a decade after the war, the last examples giving way to Avro Shackletons as late as February 1954. A few Shackletons remained on RAF strength in 1991, forty years after the first specimens were delivered.

The de Havilland Mosquito, which is unlikely to have emerged if its makers had not designed and built the civil racing Comet in 1934, was not only the most versatile type used in the Second World War, working with distinction as a light bomber, night fighter, trainer, on photographic reconnaissance and on sensitive

21

ABOVE: *The Avro Lancaster dropped by far the greatest tonnage of British bombs on Germany in the Second World War. This sole flying survivor is with the RAF Battle of Britain Memorial Flight.*

BELOW: *The main hall of the Manchester Air and Space Museum is well filled, with a 1952 Avro Shackleton as the centrepiece and, in the foreground, the exposed airframe structure of a Hawker Hunter.*

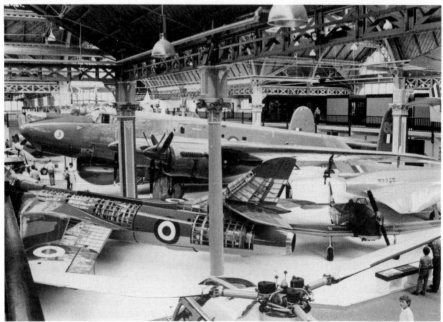

The de Havilland Mosquito was the most versatile operational aeroplane in the 1939-45 war and was unique in being made of wood. This example flies today with British Aerospace, who are successors to the original manufacturers.

high-speed communications duties, but it was unique for the 1940s in being built of wood. This reduced the pressure on the conventional sources of materials and enabled many fringe companies, such as furniture manufacturers, to play vital parts in the production process. Although many types were used to great effect between 1939 and 1945 (and the contributions to final success made by some of the less widely publicised aircraft should not be underestimated), the famous four were the Hurricane, Spitfire, Lancaster and Mosquito.

Jet-propelled aircraft are not generally associated with the Second World War, but the first Gloster Meteors entered squadron service in 1944 and were used with effect against the V-1 flying bombs that were being launched at Britain in large numbers. The first jets had poor acceleration and sluggish power response, but once they were 'wound up' they could attain creditable level speeds. As with their piston-powered predecessors, Meteors increased in speed and general performance over several years

of development, the final fighter version attaining 530 miles (853 km) per hour at an operational height of 40,000 feet (12,000 m), which was about 120 miles (193 km) per hour faster than that of the first mark. Historically, the Meteor was the first jet to join squadrons of the RAF and was the only Allied jet to see action in the Second World War.

The first jets, which from 1946 included the de Havilland Vampire, were treated in much the same manner as the piston-engined types, with units using similar cockpit checks and procedures. The pilots who flew them were accustomed to propeller-driven aircraft and even the instrument layouts were identical; several years passed before the new era of second-generation jets, in which all operating practices were reviewed and revised. A pilot from the Second World War stepping into a modern fighter would find few items that he could identify instantly.

Propellers did not, however, go out of use with the introduction of the Meteor and the Vampire; even new fighters

The first jet aircraft to enter RAF service and the only Allied one to serve operationally in the Second World War was the Gloster Meteor. This mark 7 two-seat training version was on display for several years at the now defunct Torbay Air Museum.

entered service, including the de Havilland Hornet for the RAF and the Hawker Sea Fury for the Royal Navy. The Hornet was the fastest piston-engined fighter ever used by the air force and it had the advantage of a long range and endurance at low level, a feature sadly lacking in the fuel-guzzling jets; it also had a rate of climb nearly double that of the first Meteors and it served successfully against terrorists in the Malayan jungle until June 1955. The Sea Fury lasted even longer, remaining on the strength of the Royal Naval Volunteer Reserve units until they were disbanded in 1957.

The Hawker Sea Fury was the Royal Navy's last piston-engined fleet fighter. This two-seat trainer variant was flying regularly until 1990.

The Percival Sea Prince was the last piston-engined type to be used by the Royal Navy for training air observers. This preserved specimen is owned by the appropriately styled Rural Naval Air Service based at Bourn, near Cambridge.

OLD AIRCRAFT TODAY

The preceding chapters have surveyed the progressive development of the aeroplane. Fortunately not all the early machines have been lost and there are enough examples of types of each decade to be able to study them in museums and collections all over Britain. While most of the oldest aircraft are on static exhibition only, a few fly; some, therefore, can be seen at close quarters in city centres and others can be seen in the air over particular aerodromes. There used to be argument about the merits of flying old aircraft, but most supporters of the preservation movement now agree that machines in all conditions should be exhibited, including the remains of those that have been salvaged from salt water and which can be seen almost as they were found.

If an early aeroplane is to be restored for static display, the aim may be just to present an attractive exterior regardless of the integrity of the hidden structure beneath. Sometimes, because essential components cannot be found or made, this method is the only way in which a project can be completed, but in some cases even non-flying exhibits are rebuilt authentically as nearly as possible to the original condition. When a machine is intended to fly, however, there are many problems but few options, for on the one hand as many original parts as possible must be retained and on the other hand the aircraft must be safe and fully airworthy; any doubtful components must be discarded.

Although every conscientious restorer is anxious that the aeroplane will emerge as a repaired original rather than just a new machine that has been built alongside the ashes of the old, perhaps we should think about the full meaning of the word 'original' in this context. Aircraft in daily use suffer from considerable wear and tear and many items are replaced throughout their working lives; also, a machine (especially a trainer, or one used operationally) may be damaged to the extent that a complete wing or more may need to be changed. This may happen several times before it is retired and taken over by a museum, yet no one would complain about its lack of originality at the time of the ownership change, so perhaps we worry too much about subsequent events.

Restoration is a long, slow and complex process. When an aeroplane is ac-

Before the Royal Air Force Museum was established, selected aircraft were kept at various Service stations before being collected together for display at Hendon. Upper left, a Hawker Tempest V at Abingdon in 1968; lower left, a Boulton Paul Defiant night fighter also at Abingdon; upper right, a Supermarine Walrus amphibian (known originally as the Seagull) at Campden, New South Wales, Australia; lower right, a Westland Lysander at RAF Finningley in 1961.

quired, often many items are missing and others are beyond repair. Searches for parts may be world-wide, while existing damaged pieces may need to be built up to be used solely as patterns to enable new ones to be made, for usually no drawings are available. Several years may elapse between a machine being obtained and its appearance again either on museum display or on the aerodrome flightline; the time taken is proportionately longer in the latter case, as

This Supermarine Spitfire XVI was photographed at RAF Ouston before its eventual transfer to the Royal Scottish Museum's base at East Fortune airfield, North Berwick.

26

ABOVE: *The first aircraft to arrive at the Manchester Air and Space Museum was this Miles Magister trainer of 1937 origin. Careful handling was needed to transfer it into position.*

RIGHT: *The Magister as the first occupant of the exhibition hall, which opened in 1983.*

nothing can be skimped and the Civil Aviation Authority's laid-down airworthiness standards must be met.

There are many factors to be considered by those who operate and fly early aeroplanes. The most important of these is an essential understanding of the value of an irreplaceable historic flying machine. This dictates strict control over where, when and how it is flown. Many modern airfields are unsuitable for the veterans, for long single runways are the least acceptable places from which to take off and land; because of the aircraft's weathervane tendencies, the lack of directional control when on the ground and the resulting need to be able to operate into wind, multi-directional grass sites are the best, but there are not many of these left. Most old aeroplanes are fully manageable only in almost calm conditions, so any temptation to fly when

ABOVE: *In addition to the Royal Navy's airworthy Fairey Swordfish torpedo-carrier of the Second World War, a second example is mounted in pride of place at the Fleet Air Arm Museum at Yeovilton. Behind it is a Fairey Gannet.*

BELOW: *The de Havilland Rapide (known in Service use as the Dominie) was a highly successful feeder airliner/light transport aircraft before, during and after the Second World War. Four specimens are still flying.*

The first prototype de Havilland Mosquito was built at Salisbury Hall and flew in November 1940. Here it is on public view at its birthplace, now the Mosquito Aircraft Museum.

the wind is gusting, or if the engine feels as though it is not performing well, must be resisted; it is essential, but not always easy at the time, to put the machine back in its hangar and wait until everything is in order, even though this may disappoint a large, expectant crowd of spectators. Also, no old aircraft should be flown to or near its limits; the aim must be to show the machine in its intended element, in the air, but not to place any part of the engine or airframe at an unacceptable risk.

The preservation movement is spread geographically over most of Britain and the styles of the organisations concerned are equally varied. There are the large national institutions, such as the Science Museum and the Imperial War Museum, with some very small amateur groups which satisfy the wishes of those who choose to spend their spare time on work connected with the acquisition, restoration, preservation and display of particular aircraft types that appeal to them. All

have a part to play and nearly all are in membership of the British Aviation Preservation Council, which is a national voluntarily run body that fosters the needs and interests of all concerned. Although there is some duplication of effort among these organisations, in many ways they are complementary. The Shuttleworth Collection, based on the all-grass aerodrome at Old Warden near Biggleswade in Bedfordshire, concentrates on the earliest flying machines, from a 1909 Bleriot XI to a Spitfire of the Second World War. The Imperial War Museum's Duxford site contains large numbers of heavy metal aircraft of the Second World War and beyond. These places are completely different in appearance, atmosphere and aim, but each fulfils an essential role within the historic aircraft movement.

Some organisations specialise in rescuing the remains of crashed aircraft from mountain tops and others search for them underwater, such as the recovery of a

29

Possibly the most ambitious restoration project yet tackled was the rebuilding of the Shuttleworth Collection's famous de Havilland DH88 Comet that won the Macrobertson Air Race from England to Australia in 1934.

Vickers Wellington from Loch Ness by the Royal Scottish Museum and Heriot-Watt University. Many of the smallest voluntary groups have very limited resources and they stretch these to the maximum in exhibiting their possessions outdoors, with little hope of putting them under cover.

There is plenty to see, but please remember that if these machines are to be available for future generations to admire, your entry fee, your shop purchase and perhaps even a donation will help towards that important aim.

Restoration of the Comet involved more than fifty companies in the aerospace and associated industries, but here we see the result of that support. Although owned by the Shuttleworth Collection, the famous record-breaker was restored for the benefit of the nation.

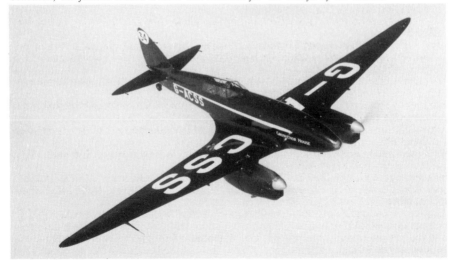

FURTHER READING

Cornwall, E. L. *Still Flying*. Ian Allan, 1979.
Howe, Stuart. *Mosquito Survivors*. Aston Publications, 1986.
Jackson, A. J. *British Civil Aircraft since 1919* (3 volumes.) Putnam, various dates to 1974.
Lewis, Peter. *British Racing and Record-breaking Aircraft*. Putnam, 1971.
March, Peter. *Preserved Aircraft*. Ian Allan, 1980.
Mulelly, Ian, and Smallwood, Hugh. *Airworthy! Flying Vintage Aircraft*. Blandford, 1981.
Ogilvy, David. *DH88: de Havilland's Racing Comets*. Airlife, 1988.
Ogilvy, David. *The Shuttleworth Collection*. Airlife, 1989.
Ogilvy, David (editor). *From Bleriot to Spitfire: Flying Historic Aeroplanes*. Airlife, 1991.
Sharp, C. Martin. *DH: A History of de Havilland*. Airlife, 1982.
Thetford, Owen. *Aircraft of the Royal Air Force since 1918*. Putnam, 1971.
Thetford, Owen. *British Naval Aircraft since 1912*. Putnam, 1982.

PLACES TO VISIT

Intending visitors are advised to find out the dates and times of opening before making a special journey. The organisations listed are all members of the British Aviation Preservation Council which can be contacted at PO Box 356, St Albans, Hertfordshire AL4 9PT.

Aerospace Museum, RAF Cosford, Shifnal, Shropshire TF11 8UP. Telephone: 090722 4872 or 4112.

Aircraft Radio Museum and Percival Collection, Coventry Airport, Baginton, Coventry, West Midlands. Telephone: 0203 302449 or 302668. By appointment.

Bomber County Aviation Museum, South Promenade, Cleethorpes, South Humberside. Telephone: 0472 696344. Summer weekends.

British Rotorcraft Museum, The Airport, Weston-super-Mare, Avon. Telephone: 0934 822524.

Brooklands Museum, Brooklands Road, Weybridge, Surrey KT13 0QN. Telephone: 0932 857381.

City of Bristol Museum and Art Gallery, Queens Road, Bristol BS8 1RL. Telephone: 0272 299771.

City of Norwich Aviation Museum, Norwich Airport, Norwich, Norfolk. By appointment.

Cornwall Aero Park, Culdrose Manor, Helston, Cornwall TR13 0GA. Telephone: 03265 3404 or 4549. Summer only.

Derby Industrial Museum, The Silk Mill, off Full Street, Derby DE1 3AR. Telephone: 0332 293111 extension 740. (Many aero engines.)

Dumfries and Galloway Aviation Museum, Former Control Tower, Heathhall Industrial Estate, Dumfries. Telephone (Secretary): 0387 53807. Weekends.

Duxford Airfield (Imperial War Museum), Duxford, Cambridge CB2 4QR. Telephone: 0223 833963.

Fleet Air Arm Museum, Royal Naval Air Station, Yeovilton, Yeovil, Somerset BA22 8HT. Telephone: 0935 840565.

Imperial War Museum, Lambeth Road, London SE1 6HZ. Telephone: 071-735 8922.

Lashenden Air Warfare Museum, Headcorn Aerodrome, Headcorn, Kent TN27 9HX. Telephone: 0622 890226. Summer weekends.

Manchester Air and Space Museum, Liverpool Road, Castlefield, Manchester M3 4FP. Telephone: 061-833 9555.

Midland Air Museum, Coventry Airport, Baginton, Coventry, West Midlands. Telephone: 0203 301033.

Mosquito Aircraft Museum, Salisbury Hall, London Colney, St Albans, Hertfordshire. Telephone: 0727 22051. Summer weekends.

Museum of Army Flying, Middle Wallop, Stockbridge, Hampshire SO20 8DY. Telephone: 0264 62121 extension 4421 or 4428.

Museum of Flight (Royal Scottish Museum), East Fortune Airfield, North Berwick, East Lothian EH39 5LF. Telephone: 062088 308.

Newark Air Museum, Winthorpe Airfield, Newark-on-Trent, Nottinghamshire NG24 2NY. Telephone: 0636 707170.

Norfolk and Suffolk Aviation Museum, Flixton, Bungay, Suffolk. Telephone: 0986 3923. Summer weekends.

North East Aircraft Museum, Washington Road, Sunderland, Tyne and Wear. Telephone: (evenings only) 091-385 4857.

Royal Air Force Museum, Grahame Park Way, Hendon, London NW9 5LL. Telephone: 081-205 2266. Displays include Bomber Command and Battle of Britain halls.

Science Museum, Exhibition Road, South Kensington, London SW7 2DD. Telephone: 071-938 8000.

Science Museum, Wroughton Airfield, Swindon, Wiltshire SN4 9NS. Telephone: 0793 814466. (Special events during summer.)

Second World War Aircraft Preservation Society, Lasham Airfield, Alton, Hampshire. Telephone: 0420 83534. Weekends.

Shuttleworth Collection, Old Warden Aerodrome, Biggleswade, Bedfordshire SG18 9ER. Telephone: 076727 288.

Southampton Hall of Aviation (incorporating the Mitchell Museum), Albert Road South, Southampton, Hampshire SO1 1FR. Telephone: 0703 635830.

South Yorkshire Aviation Society, Home Farm, Firbeck, Worksop, Nottinghamshire. Telephone: 0709 812168. By appointment.

Wales Aircraft Museum, Cardiff-Wales Airport, Rhoose, Barry, South Glamorgan CF6 9EU. Telephone: 0446 710135.

Wessex Aviation Society, The Knoll Gardens, Stapehill Road, Stapehill, Wimborne Minster, Dorset. Telephone: 0202 873931. By appointment.